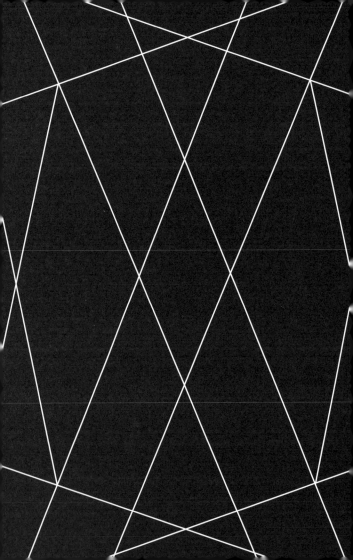

Don't Worry, Be Happy

Practical Advice for Positive Mental Well-Being

Claire Chamberlain

DON'T WORRY, BE HAPPY

An Hachette UK Company
www.hachette.co.uk

Vie Books, an imprint of Summersdale Publishers Ltd
Part of Octopus Publishing Group Limited
Carmelite House
50 Victoria Embankment
LONDON
EC4Y 0DZ
UK

www.summersdale.com

Printed and bound in Poland

ISBN: 978-1-80007-039-4

Substantial discounts on bulk quantities of Summersdale books are available to corporations, professional associations and other organizations. For details contact general enquiries: telephone: +44 (0) 1243 771107 or email: enquiries@summersdale.com.

Contents

Introduction

"Stop worrying."

How many times have you heard those words, perhaps uttered with concern, or maybe sometimes even frustration? It can seem a simple and well-meaning phrase, but the reality is that stopping worrying can be easier said than done.

Of course, we all have concerns from time to time. But when worries start to pop intrusively into our heads each and every day, they can disturb our inner peace and leave us feeling unsettled, uncomfortable and anxious. Chronic worrying can lead to stress, anxiety disorders and even depression, as our world seems to become a darker, scarier place. Deciding to "stop worrying" is all well and good – but how?

This book is designed to help you understand why worries arise and how they can get stuck in a loop in your head, before offering a series of simple steps, practical advice and inspiring words to uplift and support your well-being, and remind you there is joy to be found around every corner.

"

Have patience with
all things, but first of
all with yourself.

Francis de Sales

Now is a great time to start believing in yourself

What is Mental Health?

Mental health, also referred to as your inner well-being or emotional health, is something we all have. As you probably know, it's often in flux, sometimes changing on a daily (or even hourly) basis. You might be feeling happy and positive one moment, but if your circumstances change – for example, if you enter a period of uncertainty – worries and anxieties can start to flood your mind, disrupting your inner harmony. Often, the bad things we fear never come to pass, but if those worries have already crept in, it can feel like game over for your peace of mind.

Just as poor mental health can affect your physical state, your physical state can also affect your well-being – everything from a poor diet to a hormone imbalance can alter the way you feel about yourself and the world around you. Your mental health, then, is something that needs to be nurtured and protected. Taking responsibility for it, by making even the smallest of changes, can help you feel more empowered, resilient and better able to cope with your own personal challenges. It's never too late to do something positive for yourself.

THE MENTAL HEALTH SPECTRUM

No one is either permanently "happy and healthy" or "struggling and unwell". In fact, categorizing people in this way can have potentially harmful consequences, creating unhelpful and damaging misconceptions of mental health. Instead, it's better to think of everyone's mental health as existing on a broad spectrum. This spectrum ranges from excellent mental health, where we feel content, productive and resilient, to crisis, which includes severe symptoms such as panic attacks or depressive episodes.

Let's face it, we all have good days and bad days: times when we display resilience to life's challenges and cope well, and other times when life can seem exhausting, overwhelming and even scary. Even if you've been diagnosed with a specific mental health disorder, you will still have periods where you find you can manage your illness well, while other times will seem much harder. We will all move around on this spectrum during our lives – in fact, the World Health Organization (WHO) states that one in four of us will experience mental health difficulties at some stage in our lives. The key here is the phrase "at some stage": if you're struggling right now, know that things can (and will) change.

The impact of poor mental health

Poor mental health can impact all areas of your life. If you feel plagued by chronic worries, anxiety or depression, you'll likely have low mood, feel lacking in energy, find simple tasks overwhelming or be less interested in activities you used to enjoy. You may want to sleep a lot of the time or find you struggle to sleep at all. This can leave you feeling alone, but you're not: however bad it seems, others have been here before you. What's more, they have found a way out – and you can too.

DOUBT WHOM YOU WILL, BUT NEVER YOURSELF.

Christian Nestell Bovee

HOW ARE YOU *REALLY*?

It's time to be honest: underneath those smiling social media posts or the profile pictures you're happy to show to the world, how are you feeling *really*? Many of us are only willing to share the best bits of our lives with others, sometimes even finding it hard to admit to ourselves when we're struggling. Is there anything going on beneath the surface that you find hard to confront? Taking time to acknowledge these deeper worries or fears can help you come to terms with them, and shining a light on them can stop them seeming so scary.

Writing them down can be a creative way of addressing anything that's lurking in the back of your mind. If you don't know where to start, that's normal – stream-of-consciousness writing, or free writing, is a method whereby you pick a topic, word or feeling, and let your thoughts flow on to the page. Don't worry if you go off topic – that's part of the process – and don't concern yourself with punctuation or grammar. When you read it back to yourself, you may find you've brought to light your hidden fears or concerns.

LEARNING TO SPOT
THE WARNING SIGNS

Sadly, living in a state of chronic stress can begin to feel like the norm. But let it go on for too long and you may be at risk of burnout (a state of mental, emotional and physical exhaustion). This doesn't just happen overnight: it's the result of many months (or even years) of ignoring your body's warning signs. Fatigue, apathy, growing cynicism and feeling detached from reality are all signs of potential burnout. You may experience physical symptoms too – headaches, skin conditions (such as eczema) and IBS symptoms can all be a result of chronic stress and burnout.

WHAT CAN NEGATIVELY AFFECT YOUR MENTAL HEALTH?

There are so many factors that can influence our mental well-being. From past trauma to financial, employment or housing worries, to concerns about physical illness, relationships or bereavement – we will all face pain, upheaval and challenge in our lives. There is no right or wrong way to feel when we're hit with events and feelings like these – we will all respond differently and some may be more affected than others. Often, our response will relate to our past experiences, the strength of our support network and how we feel other areas of our life are going. When worrying events occur, it can create a spiral of anxiety and negative thinking. But if we take a little time to explore what's going on, as well as strengthening our mindset, it can help us cope more effectively in the face of adversity. Truly pinpointing the source of our worry, rather than getting lost in a sense of free-floating anxiety, can help, as can building your support network. Who might you be able to talk things through with?

YOUR PRESENT CIRCUMSTANCES DON'T DETERMINE WHERE YOU CAN GO; THEY MERELY DETERMINE WHERE YOU START.

Nido Qubein

Forgive your past mistakes

Work and financial worries

Worrying about money is a common mental-health trigger. Overdrafts, unpaid bills and maxed-out credit cards can lead to sleepless nights, as can unemployment or having to manage an irregular income. These problems can often feel so big that they seem overwhelming, but if you feel helpless, remember there are always small measures you can take. Setting yourself a daily or weekly budget, starting to pay off just one debt or seeking advice from a financial support charity are all good first steps that will add up.

Worry pretends
to be necessary,
but serves no
useful purpose.

Eckhart Tolle

LIVING OUT OF BALANCE

We often hear the word "balance" when it comes to living our lives, but what does it mean and how do we achieve it? The idea of balance is often misconstrued as meaning having to "do it all" – somehow prioritizing work, family, friends, romance, hobbies, fitness *and* relaxation time. But the truth is, "balance" means figuring out what is most important *to you*, and then adjusting your time and energy accordingly. Because of this, balance is going to look different for everybody.

Sometimes, it's only when we're living out of balance that it becomes necessary to address this issue. Generally speaking, if you're living out of balance, it means you're spending too much of your time, energy and concentration in a particular area of your life, to your own detriment. It's most common to feel unbalanced when work or chores take over our lives, leaving little space for "you time", fun and relaxation. But it's good to remember that work is an important aspect of life too, and one that can give us a sense of purpose – we need this balance in our lives to help us remain happy, healthy and fulfilled.

Do something that makes you happy today

SO MUCH TO DO, SO LITTLE TIME

"Do food shop, update spreadsheet, pay gas bill, make vet appointment, put washing on, arrange childcare, call boss…" Our to-do lists can seem never-ending, leaving little time for fun or even basic relaxation. If life has begun to feel a little out of balance, consider any small adjustments you might be able to make. Is there anything you could delegate? What genuinely needs to get done? Is there anything that can be scrapped altogether? And remember to add some down time to your to-do list too, such as a walk or a yoga class.

SOCIAL MEDIA AND MENTAL HEALTH

On the one hand, social media is a fantastic tool that can engage, energize and inspire, but on the other, it's a dangerous time-drain that has the potential to damage your self-worth. If you suspect you're experiencing the latter, it might be a good idea to consider your social media habits. How long do you spend on social sites each day? What type of content do you tend to engage with? And – most importantly – how does scrolling make you feel, both during and afterwards? Yes, drawing inspiration from others can be fun, but if you're left comparing your home, body or even life unfavourably with strangers', it might be a good idea to take a screen break or download an app that helps you limit your time on social media. And always remember, social media portrays the heavily filtered "best bits", not the ordinary, mundane or negative. After all, no one's life is Instagrammable 24/7 – and yours probably measures up just fine. If you find that certain accounts continually trigger you in a negative way, remember you can unfollow them, be it brands, influencers or even those you know in the real world. If you don't click online, it might be time to move on.

SLEEP DEPRIVATION

Worries can keep you awake at night, but the more you struggle to drift off, the greater your anxiety can become, creating a vicious cycle that can leave you feeling drained, irritable and on edge. Stress, depression and anxiety can all affect your quality of sleep, but these issues are also exacerbated by tiredness. If you struggle with insomnia, you'll know that feeling fearful of bedtime is also common. The good news is, there are steps you can take to cope, including avoiding caffeine in the afternoons, limiting or avoiding naps

and turning off the blue light emitted
from devices at least one hour before bed.
Studies also show that a warm bath or
shower an hour or two before bedtime can
help. Your body temperature will rise in
the warm water, which produces a more
pronounced dip in temperature afterwards.
This temperature drop can help you
drift off to the land of nod more easily.

Above all, don't suffer in silence –
if nothing seems to help, make an
appointment with your doctor.

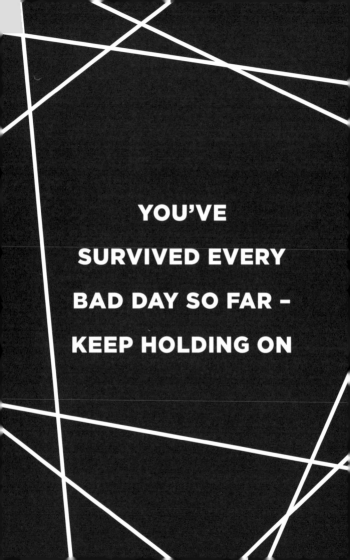

REMEMBER THE BLUE SKY. IT MAY AT TIMES BE OBSCURED BY CLOUDS, BUT IT IS ALWAYS THERE.

Andy Puddicombe

HORMONES AND MOODS

Your hormones are chemical messengers that are released by glands into your bloodstream. They influence a range of organs and bodily functions, helping to regulate everything from metabolism to mood to your reproductive cycle.

If you have periods, you will experience fluctuating hormone levels as part of your menstrual cycle, with oestrogen appearing to have an impact on levels of mood-regulating serotonin and dopamine. Premenstrual syndrome (PMS) and premenstrual dysphoric disorder (PMDD), as well as postnatal depression, are all believed to have strong hormonal components. If you notice your worry, anxiety or depression is cyclical, it can be worth keeping a mood diary alongside a menstrual cycle diary, to see if there is any correlation.

There are, of course, other causes of hormonal imbalances: they can occur due to stress, medication and nutritional deficiencies, with symptoms including mood fluctuations, fatigue, weight change and low sex drive. Getting regular exercise, eating enough protein and healthy fats, reducing the amount of sugar in your diet and getting a good night's sleep can all help to naturally regulate your hormones. If your symptoms are severe and you suspect the cause is hormonal, your GP can offer help and support.

BEWARE OF THE GAP: THE GAP BETWEEN WHERE YOU ARE AND WHERE YOU WANT TO BE. SIMPLY THINKING OF THE GAP WIDENS IT, AND YOU END UP FALLING THROUGH.

Matt Haig

Speak kindly to yourself today

PHYSICAL HEALTH WORRIES

We often compartmentalize health issues into "physical" or "mental", but the truth is there is often a huge grey area. For example, a diagnosis of a serious physical condition can bring with it huge amounts of stress, worry and anxiety. Fears for your own (and your family's) future can become crippling, and if you are suddenly unable to work, it can bring added financial pressure too.

Even a more minor or acute physical complaint can have implications for your mental health, especially if it means you have to live in pain for a while, or if an injury stops you being able to take part in your usual daily activities or fitness pursuits.

If you're worried about a physical health condition, don't put off a visit to your doctor – addressing the issue head-on is always a good idea and acting in your own best interests can give you a sense of control. And don't keep it to yourself: if you're struggling to come to terms with a diagnosis, there are trained counsellors and nurses who can offer support and advice. Ask your doctor for more information.

It's a

new day!

Approach

it with

curiosity

and wonder

Ask for help.
Not because
you are weak.
But because
you want to
remain strong.

Les Brown

THE TROUBLE WITH UNCERTAINTY

Do you struggle mentally in times of uncertainty, or find your brain gets stuck in a worry loop when external circumstances seem to constantly change? You're not alone. In evolutionary terms, stability equals security, so in an attempt to keep us "safe" our minds are often highly resistant to change. Unfortunately, as we've all experienced, curveballs will keep getting thrown our way. The interesting thing is, it's often not the circumstances that unsettle us: it's our resistance to them. Wanting everything to stay the same in times of flux can see us struggling with an internal battle that we simply can't win. By sitting with our uncomfortable feelings and figuring out a way forward, instead of clinging to the past, we can learn to work with the changes that are happening around us and even spot new opportunities. Learning to go with the flow can seem scary at first, but if you pause for just a moment and take a deep breath, you might just see a new way to move forward.

Understanding Your Mental Health

When you're feeling relaxed, calm and happy, you might not give your mental health all that much thought. After all, when everything's going smoothly, good mental health can be something we take for granted. But with one in four people likely to experience mental health problems at some point in their lives (and with one in six people living with a common mental health condition, such as anxiety), it's important to give it some thought. Alongside this is the worrying evidence that people are experiencing mental health problems at an ever-earlier age. According to The Children's

Society in the UK, the likelihood of young people having a mental health problem has risen by 50 per cent over the past three years, with 50 per cent of all mental health problems beginning at the age of just 14. It's clear then, that for all of us, a proactive and positive approach has become necessary when addressing mental health. The good news is that by understanding the things that can affect your mental health – including tiredness, poor diet, chronic stress and experiencing a traumatic event – and then by learning how to cope effectively, it can help to arm you if life gets complicated.

Worry versus anxiety

The words "worry" and "anxiety" are often used interchangeably, but there are some key psychological (and physiological) differences. Worrying tends to be purely thought-based, in relation to a specific event or problem. Anxiety, on the other hand, relates to your body's physiological response to fear: the "fight, flight or freeze" response. Anxiety can be a lot more free-floating and less specific. Because worrying thoughts can trigger anxiety, it's important to learn how to control worry, to stop it getting out of hand.

WORRYING DOESN'T STOP THE BAD STUFF FROM HAPPENING. IT JUST STOPS YOU FROM ENJOYING THE GOOD STUFF.

Karen Salmansohn

PAIN
VERSUS
SUFFERING

You've probably heard the well-known phrase, "Pain is inevitable; suffering is optional." And there is a lot of truth in it. We will all experience pain during our lives, be it physical or emotional – it is a part of the fluctuations of life. Even if you are fit, happy and healthy right now, there will be future points in your life where you will experience illness, bereavement, loss or stress. Whether we suffer because of this pain is up to us. We can choose, in every moment, how we respond to the trials thrown our way and, if we acknowledge, accept and ride out the pain we experience in life, we can often avoid a lot of the suffering (the worry, anxiety and stress) it can bring with it. At first, this might be incredibly challenging. After all, we live within a society that often conditions us to block out painful experiences, sometimes with the use of alcohol, drugs or food. But coming to terms with the fact that pain is merely a part of the interwoven fabric of living can help us to really sit with it and experience it: pain does not last forever, and without the lows, we would not be able to appreciate the joy of the highs.

INHALE DEEPLY,

EXHALE SLOWLY.

REPEAT

HOW TO
SPOT ANXIETY

Anxiety tends to be characterized by feelings of worry, often in relation to a future or imagined event. In these instances, our brains seem to be programmed to tune into only the worst-case scenarios, and we can find ourselves in a state of dread or panic at the thought of whatever it is we're worried about. Anxiety can bring with it a range of symptoms, including agitation, a racing heart and nausea. Think you might be suffering from anxiety? Grounding yourself in the present moment, by focusing on what you can see, hear and feel right now, can help.

Is it depression?

Depression will affect people in different ways, but there are certain characteristics beyond simply feeling low or unhappy that can help you figure out if you're suffering from this condition. Commonly, people report feeling a sense of emptiness or hopelessness, as well as a loss of interest in activities and hobbies they once enjoyed. Depression can often go hand in hand with worry and anxiety, but it doesn't necessarily have to. If you think you're being affected by depression, try to open up to someone you trust. If chatting in person or on the phone feels too hard, you could put your feelings down in an email to someone you trust.

**SOME
ROSES GROW
THROUGH
CONCRETE.
REMEMBER THAT.**

Brandi L. Bates

THE IMPACT OF TRAUMA

Experiencing or witnessing a traumatic event can have a profound impact on your mental health. For example, if you have ever experienced abuse or assault, been in an accident, been caught up in warfare, experienced a traumatic birth, or had a near-death experience – anything that has caused extreme fear, horror or a sense of helplessness – you may experience post-traumatic stress disorder (PTSD). Common symptoms include vivid flashbacks, nightmares, intrusive thoughts, feeling hyper-vigilant, anxiety, panic attacks and feeling emotionally shut down. Depending on the trauma, you may also experience physical symptoms, such as pain or nausea. Opening up to someone you trust may help and, if you want professional support, speak with your doctor about getting a referral for talking therapy, such as cognitive behavioural therapy (CBT). This type of treatment has proven to be highly effective for those suffering with PTSD, because it holds a space for the patient to make sense of their experiences, as well as helping them to develop self-management techniques. One study has even found that talking therapy might create biological changes in patients, hinting at the fact that the damage to the brain associated with PTSD might, in fact, be reversible.

Self-Care and How to Practise It

Self-care refers to the practice of actively taking the time to care for yourself. It encompasses a wide range of activities, from looking after your physical health (through good nutrition, exercise and rest), to your mental, emotional and spiritual health (with practices such as meditation and mindfulness, yoga and journaling). It can mean realizing when you need a rest and doing something nice for yourself, such as taking a walk through nature or running yourself a warm bath with essential oils. Crucially, though, self-care is deliberate: it's about acts that consciously focus on filling your own cup. These acts don't have to be big, either – even drinking a glass of water can be an act of self-care, if it is done mindfully and with the intention of nurturing your body.

The biggest barrier to self-care is often guilt. Feeling bad about tending to your own needs is common, especially if you are a caregiver for others (such as children or relatives), or you feel you should be doing something more "productive". But remember, looking after your own mental and physical well-being will ultimately leave you with more energy to give to others, not less. So, drop the guilt – self-care is necessary.

WHY IS SELF-CARE IMPORTANT?

Self-care is a great way of positively taking responsibility for your own health. By making sure you take a little time out for yourself each day, you will likely experience greater relaxation and joy, and be better able to manage stress levels when things get overwhelming. Of course, when life starts to get hectic, self-care is often the first thing we drop – we're very good at prioritizing everyone else's needs above our own! Which is why consciously making time for self-care is so important: your mental and physical health matters just as much as anything else.

I have met myself
and I am going to
care for her fiercely.

Glennon Doyle

Today is a fresh start – embrace it fully

Start small

If you're new to self-care, you'll be
pleased to hear it doesn't have to be
expensive or time-consuming – far
from it! It doesn't take much to start
consciously looking after yourself and,
while a day at a spa is an amazing
and luxurious treat, acts of self-care
can be much smaller. Savouring a hot
cup of tea, writing in a journal for five
minutes, taking a few deep breaths or
going for a short ten-minute stroll are
all simple acts of self-care.

WHY
FITNESS
MATTERS

Many people often think of their mental and physical health as two separate systems, but it's not as clear cut as that. In fact, your mental well-being and physical fitness exist together in a close, symbiotic relationship. In short, look after your body and, more often than not, the mind will follow. There are several reasons why taking care of your body through good diet and exercise has such a profound effect on your mental health. Physiological changes, such as improved strength and stamina, can help you appreciate what you're truly capable of, building a resilience that then spills over into other areas of your life. Following a fitness regime – even committing to exercising just three times a week – gives you a steady routine, which can give you something positive to focus your energy on. And finally, working up a good old-fashioned sweat is one of the best ways to boost endorphins (feel-good hormones) in your body, giving you an instant happiness hit.

Embarking on a fitness regime can seem daunting if you haven't exercised in a while, but don't be put off. Remember, everyone who works out was a beginner once – now it's your turn to see what all the fuss is about!

GET MOVING!

While all exercise is great for your body, there's something about a cardiovascular workout (one that really gets your heart pumping) that's great for helping you push your worries to one side. Throwing yourself into a more strenuous pursuit often takes effort and concentration, which tends to take your mind off the things that have been bothering you, plus as your fitness and endurance improve, you might start to feel as though you can handle anything that comes your way – that "top of the world" feeling! So, whatever you choose to do – be it a run, cycle, swim, dance or HIIT class – it's time to get moving.

YOU CAN'T STOP
THE WAVES,
BUT YOU CAN
LEARN TO SURF.

Jon Kabat-Zinn

DO SOMETHING THAT SCARES YOU

It can sound counter-intuitive, but doing something that pushes you outside of your comfort zone can actually be a great way to ease your worries. In fact, more and more people are turning to action sports as a way to manage their anxiety – and with good reason. Anxiety is characterized physiologically by an increase in adrenaline and cortisol in the body, and one of the best ways to release this is to use it in the way it was meant to be used! Many people report feelings of deep calm and contentment after taking part in a new and adrenaline-fuelled activity that appeals to their soul. From horse riding to bouldering, surfing to open-water swimming, self-care doesn't always have to be relaxing in the traditional sense of the word. When looking to take up an action sport, always seek guidance from a qualified instructor. And remember, it's OK to start small and overcome your own personal hurdles, rather than copying other people's versions of "extreme": a long hike, bike ride or circus skills class all count if it pushes you out of your comfort zone and gives you that buzz.

Step into today with courage and positivity

Work on your strength

As with cardio workouts, strength training (such as lifting weights or Pilates) is a great way to challenge and improve both your physical and mental fitness. Many people find the routine of a strength workout – counting out reps and sets of exercises – calming for their mind. And, as well as building physical strength, you might also be improving your mental resilience. To avoid injury, good technique is everything here, so work with a personal trainer or get advice from a gym when you're getting started.

DRINK PLENTY OF WATER

It's recommended that we drink between six to eight glasses (1.6–2 litres/2.5–3.5 pints) of water a day and, while that sounds achievable, how often do you actually do it? The constant juggle of life can mean we often forget to sip regularly throughout the day, but even mild dehydration can negatively impact your mood and emotional state, making you feel sluggish and even triggering anxiety. If you often forget, set reminders on your phone, or keep a bottle of water on your desk or in your bag while out and about. Staying well-hydrated is a simple act of self-care and it's easy to turn it into a habit.

WE NEED TO
DO A BETTER
JOB OF PUTTING
OURSELVES
HIGHER ON
OUR OWN
"TO DO" LIST.

Michelle Obama

EAT WELL

In an ideal world, we'd all eat foods that fuelled and nourished our bodies optimally all of the time. After all, we know the foods that are good for us and the ones we should reserve for an occasional treat. The reality, though, is far more complex, and often our diet (and even appetite) is intrinsically linked to our emotions. For example, when you're feeling worried or anxious, how often have you found yourself reaching for a treat without thinking? If this is the case, you're not alone. In times of mental crisis, it's easy to seek an immediate and often unconscious pick-me-up in the form of sugary or fatty comfort foods. Unfortunately, soon after will come the inevitable sugar crash, leaving you feeling low, irritable and anxious all over again. Breaking the habit can seem hard, but take it one small step at a time: start with swapping your unhealthy snacks for more nourishing ones – avocado or peanut butter on toast, for example. Then, aim to cook yourself a delicious and nutritious dinner from scratch several times a week – something that fills you with joy and happiness. Think colourful, spicy curries, hearty wholesome soups and bright, zingy salads. *Bon appétit!*

Limit your caffeine intake

It can be worth keeping a food diary for a few weeks, to see if there's a connection between what you eat and drink, and your worries or anxiety. Caffeine, for example, is well known for fuelling the jitters, and sometimes an anxiety trigger can simply be physiological, such as the effects of your morning latte as the caffeine boosts your adrenaline levels, affecting your heart rate and blood pressure. Try a soothing mint tea instead and see if you notice a difference in your mood.

In the midst
of movement
and chaos,
keep stillness
inside of you.

Deepak Chopra

AROMATHERAPY

Essential oils have long been used in alternative therapies to help rebalance both body and mind, with several studies demonstrating that certain oils, including lavender and sweet orange, can help to reduce feelings of anxiety and stress. So, give your well-being a boost with some of your favourite scents. Start your day with a zingy citrus shower gel to perk up your senses, or try adding a few drops of essential oil to a warm bath at the end of the day (lavender, ylang ylang and chamomile oils are known for their calming properties). Bliss.

SPEND TIME IN NATURE

Spending time in nature offers a host of well-documented mental health benefits, including reducing stress, easing anxiety and even helping to alleviate depression. Indeed, the Japanese tradition of *shinrin-yoku* (forest bathing) is now being embraced by Western cultures, as we look to the natural world to help improve our mental health, and there are countless studies, alongside anecdotal evidence, that demonstrate time spent in green spaces is better for our well-being than time spent indoors or in an urban environment.

The practice simply involves immersing yourself in nature by walking slowly through (or sitting quietly in) an area of natural beauty and experiencing it with all of your senses. It's not just about what you can see, but about what you can smell, hear and feel. A forest or woodland setting is perfect, but any wild, natural space, such as a meadow, seashore or even parkland will do your mind and soul the world of good. Simply absorb its beauty and allow yourself to get lost in the everyday wonders that so often pass us by – you'll be amazed at how rejuvenating it can feel.

Get muddy

When it comes to nature, you don't have to simply view it from afar – you can immerse yourself in it too. Researchers have found that a type of friendly bacteria that lives in soil activates brain cells to produce serotonin – a key hormone related to mood regulation and well-being. So, don't be afraid to get your hands dirty – why not try a spot of gardening, sit with your feet in the bare earth, or make like a child and play in the mud!

BE THE WEIRDO WHO DARES TO ENJOY.

Elizabeth Gilbert

SLOW DOWN

Taking a conscious step back from your busy way of life is a wonderful way to protect your mental health, giving you more time to focus on your well-being and helping to alleviate stress. Often, a few small tweaks to your day can help you slow down: try taking your full lunch break instead of grabbing a sandwich on the go, swapping your smartphone for a book and going to bed half an hour earlier each night. You'll be amazed at what these simple changes can do for your soul.

Accept this moment, just as it is

Learn to say "no"

Do you find yourself agreeing to take on additional work, tasks and responsibilities without stopping to think how these extra demands on your time will impact your life? So often we find ourselves juggling more than we want to, simply because we're too polite to say "no". But taking on too many projects can cause your stress and worry levels to soar. Next time someone asks you for a favour that involves giving up your precious time, stop and consider whether it's something you can really take on before agreeing. It's OK to say "no" sometimes.

WHEN YOU ARE SAYING "YES" TO OTHERS, MAKE SURE YOU ARE NOT SAYING "NO" TO YOURSELF.

Paulo Coelho

Hang in there – you can do this

TRY JOURNALING

Journaling has become something of an art form in recent years and there are so many different types out there – from bullet journals to gratitude journals – that you'll likely find something to suit your style. Most of us aren't in the habit of writing down our innermost thoughts regularly, so it might feel odd at first. Go with it, though – many people swear by journaling to help them gain clarity and perspective, and there are no hard and fast rules. You don't need anything fancy to start, either – just a pen and notebook, and you're good to go!

Read a good book

If you find yourself lost in worrying or anxious thoughts, try immersing yourself in the pages of a great novel instead. Researchers have found that getting lost in an absorbing book can actually lower stress levels, due to the fact that reading offers a dose of healthy escapism from everyday life. Not into reading? An audiobook can be just as engrossing, and listening to someone read to you can be extra comforting. Perhaps it's time to start that new bestseller?

YOU DESERVE

TO FEEL JOYFUL

TRY COLD THERAPY

It might sound unpleasant, but taking a cold-water dip is an amazing way to get an instant mood boost. A growing tribe of cold-water swimmers are extolling the virtues of sea, river or lake swimming due to the numerous health benefits, including boosted immunity and circulation. It's also known anecdotally to help promote good mental health – and now research is providing confirmation, with scientists alluding to the fact that "cross-adaptation" is responsible for the prolonged benefits to the mind. The theory is that the more often you swim, the less your body begins to react to the shock of the cold water and this in turn can make you less reactive to everyday stress.

When outdoor swimming, safety is paramount, so make sure you are fully prepared and always follow safety guidelines, including using a tow float and never swimming alone. You don't need to leap into the great outdoors to reap the benefits though – simply turning the temperature to cool for 30 seconds at the end of your shower can give you the same glow. (Be mindful of health conditions, especially relating to the heart, and always consult your doctor if you have concerns.)

Look deep into
nature, and then
you will understand
everything better.

Albert Einstein

Do what makes your soul sing

JOIN A CLUB

Finding something you enjoy and doing it as part of a like-minded group is a great way to engender a feeling of belonging, which is key to well-being and good mental health. Whatever you're into – be it a team sport, running, art, reading, knitting – you'll likely find a club out there for you. The great thing these days is, even if there's nothing local, you'll no doubt find an online group for support. Joining a club can seem intimidating, but that sense of connection will be worth the pay-off and your hobby is a great focal point if you're nervous.

You are

stronger

than you

realize

TRY
MEDITATION

If you're prone to worry, meditation can be a powerful tool to help calm your mind. At its essence, meditation is simply focused attention, without judgement. Research shows the positive benefits of a regular meditation practice include reduced stress and anxiety, so it's perfect if your mind is often racing.

To get started, find a quiet place where you won't be disturbed, gently close your eyes and draw your attention to the rise and fall of your breath. Notice the rhythm of your breathing, without judgement – is it slow and deep, or fast and shallow? After a few moments, you might like to start counting your breaths – as you breathe in, count "one", as you breathe out, count "two", and so on until you reach ten. Then start again from one. If your mind starts to wander, simply acknowledge your thoughts without judgement, then start counting from one again. When you first start out, aim to follow your breath for 5 minutes; you can slowly build this up as you become used to the practice. Guided meditations are a wonderful entry point – you can find these online or via a meditation app.

YOU ARE

EXACTLY WHERE

YOU NEED TO BE

RIGHT NOW

PLEDGE THAT YOU
WILL LOOK IN
THE MIRROR AND
FIND THE UNIQUE
BEAUTY IN YOU.

Tyra Banks

LIVE IN THE MOMENT

Have you ever noticed that your worries tend to centre on things that have happened in the past or situations that might occur in the future? Rarely, if ever, are we worried about things that are happening *right now*. That's because we are able to handle each and every moment as it arises, because if action is needed, we will be in a position to take it. This is the main principle of living more mindfully – keeping our minds focused on the present moment, which is the only moment we ever have. Everything else – constant replays of the past or fears for the future – does not actually exist in the physical world. Whenever you find your mind wandering or feeling anxious, bring yourself back to the present by taking a moment to focus on your senses – what can you see *right now*? What sounds can you hear? Are there any smells? Can you feel the ground beneath your feet or the chair you are sitting on? Grounding yourself through your senses can be highly effective and can help to lessen worries.

BREATHE.
LET GO.
AND REMIND
YOURSELF
THAT THIS VERY
MOMENT IS THE
ONLY ONE YOU
KNOW YOU HAVE
FOR SURE.

Oprah Winfrey

Sip a cup of tea

There's an excellent reason why many of us pour a cup of tea in times of stress: studies have shown tea drinking can have a similar effect on the brain as meditation, stimulating the alpha brainwaves associated with relaxation. There are so many different varieties of tea to choose from, so why not experiment? Black and green teas contain high levels of the amino acid L-theanine, known to increase dopamine levels, which can help to induce a feeling of peace. Or try soothing chamomile, which has been shown to promote a feeling of calm. Just be aware of the caffeine content of whatever you choose!

PUT IT INTO PERSPECTIVE

When you're in the middle of a stressful situation it can feel like the end of the world (or at the very least, it can ruin your day). But how many stressful scenarios have you been in previously that have actually worked themselves out? And how many times have you wished you'd spent less time fretting over something that turned out to be nothing? It's amazing how much time we spend worrying about things that always seem to turn out OK in the end.

So, next time you find yourself lost in a cycle of worry, ask yourself, will I still be worried about this next week? How about next month or next year? Will this still be a big deal in five years' time? Is it, in fact, something that you could let go of *right now*? Zooming out in this way is a simple and effective technique that can help to stop your fears and worries spiralling out of control. Sometimes, a little perspective can work wonders.

You're doing great

EMBRACE
WABI-SABI

Life will never be perfect. However you're feeling right now, this moment will pass, in the constant ebb and flow of life. This is completely normal, and acknowledging this state of flux – as well as accepting the imperfection of life – can help us feel at peace. The Japanese culture of *wabi-sabi* encourages us to focus on the beauty of imperfection; to peacefully acknowledge life exactly as it is. Next time you feel anxiety rising, accept that feelings and emotions rise and fade, and embrace the beauty of the moment, storm clouds and all.

We spend precious hours fearing the inevitable. It would be wise to use that time adoring our families, cherishing our friends and living our lives.

Maya Angelou

Do some yoga

Yoga has long been associated with feelings of peace and well-being, with research supporting its benefits. But you don't have to engage in an hour-long daily practice to reap the benefits – even just a couple of *asanas* (poses) in the morning or evening can be enough to help you unwind. *Asanas* such as downward-facing dog and cat-cow are good at invoking a sense of calm and relaxation. If you're just starting out, it's important to seek guidance from a qualified yoga instructor who will be able to teach you how to perform the poses safely. Why not join a beginners' class?

REPEAT AFFIRMATIONS

Many people are sceptical about the power of affirmations, without realizing that they probably already use them to great effect every day. If you regularly tell yourself you're a stressed person, or you are unattractive/unworthy/unlovable/not good enough – and you have started to believe this – that's affirmation in action. Isn't it funny how we're often willing to believe the negative things we tell ourselves, yet find it hard to believe anything good?

So, stop affirming negative things about yourself. Now's a great time to start with one positive affirmation each day. "I can handle whatever this day brings" or "I am enough" are good examples. Keep your affirmations short and to the point, as this will help you to repeat and align with your intention throughout the day. Why not write down your affirmations on sticky notes, so you can place them around your home to act as uplifting reminders throughout the day? Pop them on your bedside table, the bathroom mirror and even the front door, so you get a positive boost each time you leave the house.

It's OK
to say "no"
sometimes

BE PROACTIVE

Accepting and facing a worry, rather than burying your head in the sand, can be the key to easing anxiety. Try breaking down seemingly overwhelming problems into smaller, more manageable tasks. For example, if your workload is contributing to your worries, think about how you can begin to manage it more productively – what's the most pressing item on your to-do list? Can you focus on that, and that alone, for the next hour? Are there any tasks you can delegate? Remember, taking even just one small step is more positive than wasting energy worrying about the big picture.

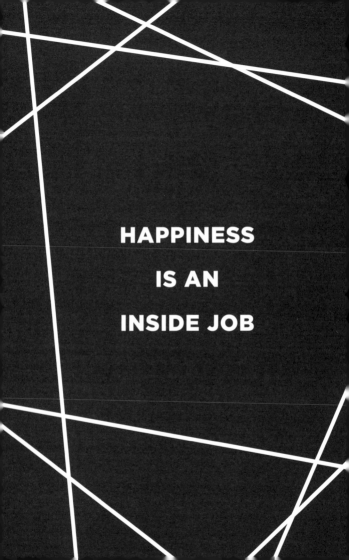

HAPPINESS

IS AN

INSIDE JOB

JOY DOES NOT
SIMPLY HAPPEN
TO US. WE HAVE
TO CHOOSE
JOY AND KEEP
CHOOSING IT
EVERY DAY.

Henri Nouwen

HAVE A MASSAGE

Easing your worries away with a relaxing massage can be highly therapeutic. Studies show that massage can be effective at reducing stress and anxiety, by providing relief from physical tension and promoting well-being. The hands-on contact is also grounding, drawing your attention out of the mind and into the body. Booking a session with a registered massage practitioner is a great idea, but if this isn't an option, a massage from a loved one can be wonderfully relaxing. Or have a go at self-massage: try massaging your scalp, by rubbing your fingertips over it in small circular motions; and work on your shoulders by rotating them slowly, then reaching across your back and drawing your fingers up and over your shoulders on both sides. And don't forget your ears! You might not traditionally associate them with massage, but gently pulling and rubbing your ear lobes can stimulate the nerve endings, resulting in the release of endorphins. During your massage, pay attention to how your body feels and visualize any stress melting away.

Try a reiki session

An alternative therapy with Japanese origins, reiki is commonly referred to as energy healing and is said to involve the transfer of universal energy from the practitioner's palms to your body, in order to regulate the flow of "life force energy". The practice is non-contact, meaning the practitioner will hover their hands above your body without touching you, and you do not need to remove any clothing. While the effectiveness of the practice is hard to prove in scientific terms, many proponents report feelings of warmth and security during a session, and a lasting sense of relaxation afterwards.

The present moment is where everything unfolds – focus on the here and now

HAVE A LAUGH

It's no joke: getting a fit of the giggles might be just what the doctor ordered when it comes to releasing tension and melting away worries. Studies show that there are numerous ways in which laughter can help to alleviate stress. For a start, a good belly laugh stimulates and then calms your stress response, heart rate and blood pressure, resulting in a feeling of peace. And that tension in your body? Laughter might just melt it away, as it boosts circulation and promotes muscle relaxation. It could be time to pop on your favourite comedy box set.

IF YOU WANT TO CONQUER THE ANXIETY OF LIFE, LIVE IN THE MOMENT, LIVE IN THE BREATH.

Amit Ray

REMEMBER, YOU ARE NOT YOUR THOUGHTS

You have thousands of thoughts each day, many of them unconscious or automatic. That's a lot of internal chatter to contend with, and if you tried to identify with each and every thought, you would drive yourself to distraction. But that's what most of us do all the time – we have a thought and we believe it to be true. Then what happens? Our mind starts to come up with a counter argument or an alternative, and we begin to question ourselves. This constant stream of thought, with all its back-and-forth arguments, can be a great source of worry and anxiety, as we buy into everything our mind tells us. But here's the thing: you are not your thoughts. You are simply the stillness beneath your thoughts, watching them as they come and go. And if you can view them like that – a bit like cars passing in front of you – watching them go without forming an attachment to them, it can help to create a little more stillness in your mind.

Embrace your creative side

Embarking on a new creative project can be deeply satisfying, and focusing your attention on making, creating, designing or building is a great way to calm your mind. As humans, we are all intrinsically creative – even if you don't view yourself as a creative person, you most definitely are. Creativity takes many forms, from painting, drawing, colouring, sculpting, film and photography, to sewing, knitting, baking, writing, singing, dancing and acting. Remember, the joy lies in the doing, not the finished outcome, so shed those inhibitions and embrace the joy of creativity – and the accompanying inner peace.

What art offers is space – a certain breathing room for the spirit.

John Updike

Your smile will create a ripple of kindness today

CALL A FRIEND

If you've been keeping quiet about your worries, opening up to even just one person can feel like a release, so why not pick up the phone and have a good old-fashioned chat with a friend? You will get a much greater sense of connection by speaking with them, as opposed to resorting to messages or emails, as your conversation will have the space to take twists and turns, and offer you the opportunity to laugh and vent with someone who understands you.

The only way to
make sense out of
change is to plunge
into it, move with it,
and join the dance.

Alan Watts

IT'S NOT THE EVENT BUT YOUR RESPONSE THAT MATTERS

Give back

When we get caught up in our own worries, we often forget that other people have struggles and problems too. Performing a selfless act to offer support and kindness to someone else will not only help them, but can often help you gain perspective in your own life. Those who spend time volunteering often report a strong sense of purpose, as well as increased happiness and confidence. Is there a project, cause or campaign you care about that you could help out with? You might be surprised by just how many people in your local community could do with a little kindness.

THERE ARE
TWO WAYS OF
SPREADING
LIGHT: TO BE THE
CANDLE OR THE
MIRROR THAT
REFLECTS IT.

Edith Wharton

THREE GOOD THINGS

There is so much doom and gloom reported in the news each day, invoking feelings of worry and fear, that we can often feel we have nothing to be thankful for. But, actually, if we look closely, most of us will be able to find lots of things to be grateful for in our lives. This is why gratitude is a powerful and radical act of self-care – if we actively seek out things to feel grateful for, and express this gratitude openly and reverently, we can rise above the fearmongering and negativity, and inspire others to approach life with this positive attitude too. Take the time to write down three things you are grateful for at the end of each day – it can be as simple as a sunny sky, a fulfilling meal or a smile. Or start a ritual with your family or friends whereby you each talk about the thing you are most grateful for over a shared meal. Remember, gratitude is the expression of appreciation – and we all have things we appreciate in life.

IT'S NOT ABOUT HOW MUCH WE HAVE, BUT HOW MUCH WE ENJOY, THAT MAKES HAPPINESS.

Charles Spurgeon

You are important, worthy and loved

Each setback is a chance to return stronger

Asking for help isn't
a sign of weakness,
it's a sign of strength.

Barack Obama

Seeking Help

If you're struggling to manage your worries and anxieties on your own, seeking support – either from someone close to you or from a professional – is an important step. So many people put on a brave face, going about their daily lives while hiding their inner turmoil beneath the surface, which can feel like a huge burden. But you don't have to do this – and you don't have to face your fears alone. When you open up, you might be surprised by how much of what you say resonates with others, and it can start an honest, straightforward and much-needed conversation about mental health.

There's no denying that telling someone you're struggling with worries, anxiety or depression can be difficult. So, choose a time when you won't be disturbed and tell just one person (it can be easier than opening up to a group). While you can't predict how they will respond, it's likely they will be concerned yet supportive. There can be a sense of relief once you've spoken your worries out loud, which can have a positive impact on your mental health in itself.

SOMETIMES, YOU HAVE TO FALL TO THE BOTTOM IN ORDER TO MAKE YOUR WAY BACK TO THE TOP AGAIN.

Bryony Gordon

PROFESSIONAL HELP: TAKING THE FIRST STEP

If you don't feel you can open up to someone you know personally or if you suspect you may need professional support – for example, in the form of a talking therapy or medication – the best starting point is to book a chat with your doctor. They will listen to your concerns in a safe and confidential environment, and should be able to offer advice or refer you for more specialist support, such as cognitive behavioural therapy (CBT) or counselling.

Counselling: what to expect

Counselling is an umbrella term used to describe a range of talking therapies, but it's also a therapy in its own right. A counsellor will listen non-judgmentally as you open up about your fears, worries and anxieties. Unlike some other therapies, a counsellor will not offer advice or suggest solutions, but will simply hold the space for you to talk freely, asking questions and prompting you to work through your issues. Many people find that being able to air their worries in this way is highly beneficial, and can provide clarity and perspective.

THE TRIUMPH CAN'T BE HAD WITHOUT THE STRUGGLE.

Wilma Rudolph

WHAT IS CBT?

Cognitive behavioural therapy (CBT) is a talking therapy that's designed to help you understand and change negative or unhelpful thoughts and/or behaviours. It's very much a collaborative process between you and your therapist, requiring commitment and dedication on your part to actively bring about positive change, and will usually involve a series of sessions, after which you'll have developed your own set of coping strategies. There are numerous studies that point toward the effectiveness of CBT as a means of treating common mental health problems and it appears to be especially effective for treating anxiety.

The way I see it,
if you want the
rainbow, you gotta
put up with the rain.

Dolly Parton

What is peer support?

Peer support involves people with lived experience of a particular condition coming together to offer support and advice to others facing the same (or similar) worries. It differs from more traditional professional support in that there is no one "expert" on hand to offer advice; instead, everyone is invited to share their experiences and insights for the benefit of others. It's often offered in a group setting and can be accessed via your health professional. You can also find peer support programmes online, or groups may be available within your local community or from student services, if you're still in education.

HELPLINES AND ONLINE CHAT SERVICES

If the thought of opening up to somebody you know makes you uncomfortable, there are plenty of places where you can gain anonymous support and advice. Helplines, such as Samaritans, provide a safe scenario for you to talk through any anxieties or problems you may be experiencing, and there is also a wealth of information available online. This includes mental health websites and online forums, where you can anonymously chat with others. When seeking online support, be mindful of the source of the information you are accessing. It's important to visit reputable sites only, for example, registered charities. Bear in mind that responsible sites will always contain trigger warnings (statements at the top of the page, warning readers about potentially upsetting or disturbing content), which can help to keep you safe if you're feeling particularly vulnerable. Another great source of support – which can help to cement and instil regular self-care practices such as mindfulness, meditation or yoga – is phone apps. Take a look to see what appeals most to you – downloading one that you can access easily on your phone can help to keep you grounded in times of worry.

IF SOMETHING
IS WRONG, FIX
IT IF YOU CAN.
BUT TRAIN
YOURSELF NOT
TO WORRY.
WORRY NEVER
FIXES ANYTHING.

Mary Hemingway

Keep
being
brave

YOUR PERSONAL ACTION PLAN

If you currently feel like you're managing your worry, stress and/or anxiety well, it can be a good idea to jot down what's working for you, so that if you experience moments of crisis in the future, you can refer back to your notes and begin your tried-and-trusted "action plan". This action plan will be personal to you, so write down anything and everything that you think may help. It could be a reminder to drink a glass of water each time you step into your kitchen; to perform three yoga poses as soon as you get out of bed in the morning; or to log back into that meditation app on your phone and return to a regular practice. You could note down people who you can call for support in moments where you feel you're struggling to cope, or a list of things that spark joy for you: a 10-minute stroll, a bunch of flowers or a chat with a loved one. Re-read your personal plan whenever you're feeling anxious, worried or low – and then *act* on it. Remember, it's always a good moment to invest a little time in yourself.

You will get there, one step at a time

RUN AS FAR AS YOU CAN IN THE DIRECTION OF YOUR BEST AND HAPPIEST DREAMS ACROSS THE BRIDGE THAT WAS BUILT BY YOUR OWN DESIRE TO HEAL.

Cheryl Strayed

Conclusion

Hopefully the information and ideas within these pages have helped you feel a little less alone, and better equipped to manage bouts of worry and anxiety as and when they arise. As well as arming you with self-care ideas to try when you're feeling low or anxious. The key message is this: difficult times will arise, but eventually they will pass. During the storms, learning how to change your mindset, rather than constantly fighting those storms or getting caught in spirals of worry, can profoundly impact the way you feel and can help you ride out the bad weather until sunnier times return.

Whatever you're going through right now, you can handle it, so keep believing in yourself, and never be afraid to ask for help from those around you. After all, it's more fun dancing in the rain with someone by your side.

Resources

For readers in the United Kingdom:

Anxiety UK: This charity provides information, support and understanding for those living with anxiety disorders. **anxietyuk.org.uk**

CALM: The Campaign Against Living Miserably (CALM) is leading a movement against male suicide. **thecalmzone.net**

Mind: This mental health charity offers support and advice to help empower anyone experiencing a mental health issue. **mind.org.uk**

Samaritans: A 24-hour, free, confidential helpline, to support you whatever you're going through. **samaritans.org; call 116 123; or email jo@samaritans.org (UK) or jo@samaritans.ie (Ireland)**

SANEline: A national, out-of-hours mental health helpline, offering specialist emotional support, guidance and information. **sane.org.uk; or email support@sane.org.uk**

For readers in the United States:

Anxiety & Depression Association of America: Education, training and research for anxiety, depression and related disorders. **adaa.org**

Freedom From Fear: A national non-profit mental health advocacy organization, helping to positively impact the lives of all those affected by anxiety, depression and related disorders. **freedomfromfear.org**

Mental Health America: promoting the overall mental health of all Americans. **mhanational.org**

Mental Health Foundation: A non-profit charitable organization specializing in mental health awareness, education, suicide prevention and addiction. **mentalhealthfoundation.org**

National Suicide Prevention Line: A 24/7 free, confidential support service for those in distress, as well as crisis resources for loved ones. **suicidepreventionlifeline.org; or call 1-800-273-8255**

Have you enjoyed this book?
If so, why not write a review on your
favourite website?

If you're interested in finding out more
about our books, find us on Facebook at
Summersdale Publishers, on Twitter at
@Summersdale and on Instagram at
@summersdalebooks and get in touch.
We'd love to hear from you!

Thanks very much for buying this
Summersdale book.

www.summersdale.com